A HISTORY OF STOURBRIDGE
NATIONAL SPIRITUALIST CHURCH

A History of
Stourbridge National
Spiritualist Church

by

Eric Hatton MSNU

PP
**Psychic Press
Limited**

Published by
Psychic Press Limited
Hertfordshire, England.
pneditorials@gmail.com

ISBN 978-0-9573322-0-1

Printed by
Lightning Source
www.lightningsource.com

Author's Foreword

From the beginning of recorded history there have been gifted individuals known as sensitives, or mediums, who have provided proof of survival beyond death to those who have been bereaved. There are also countless records of prophets and seers whose predictions have come to pass.

However, it was as a result of events in 1848, which took place in the small American hamlet of Hydesville, that Modern Spiritualism was born. Two sisters, Catherine and Margaretta Fox, had established intelligent communication with the discarnate spirit of a murdered peddler, and as knowledge and awareness of survival beyond the grave spread across America, Spiritualist churches were quickly established despite opposition from mainstream religions of the day.

Whilst we in Stourbridge cannot claim to have been among the earliest churches to spring up in the UK, my research shows that from the beginning of the 20th century a group of like-minded people met regularly to discuss the philosophy of Spiritualism and demonstrate the phenomena of mediumship.

In carrying out my research for this book I have been indebted to Ron Pratt, Cissie Shaw, Mary Simmonds, Marjorie and Harry Saich, James Grainger, my sister Laura Fisher and my late wife Heather, all of whom have contributed information and reminded me of incidents which are now contained in this book.

Nevertheless, without Sue Farrow's patient guidance, and her compiling and editing of material, *A History of Stourbridge National Spiritualist Church* would not have come to fruition.

Eric Hatton
Stourbridge, July 2012

Editor's Introduction

Stourbridge National Spiritualist Church is widely regarded as one of the jewels in the crown of British Spiritualism. Founded in 1926 – when the possibility of communication with the so-called dead was far less readily accepted than it is today – the church gave a platform to mediums and speakers of the highest quality, presenting irrefutable evidence of survival beyond death to all who came through its doors.

Throughout much of that time it has been led by Eric Hatton who, coincidentally, was born in the year of the church's founding, and first visited it in 1947 following the death of his much-loved brother. The evidence he received on that occasion, from a youthful Gordon Higginson, brought him a certainty of life after death so complete that in the many years which have followed he has become one of the Spiritualist movement's most credible and respected advocates.

Under Eric's leadership, carried out with the unstinting support of his wife Heather until her passing in 2007, the original church has been extended no less than three times to accommodate its ever-growing membership, and has become a beacon of excellence in mediumship and philosophical speaking. To this day, mediums and speakers aspire to work on the platform at Stourbridge and consider it something of an accolade to be invited to do so.

It is commonplace to see the church full to capacity, and for each and every member of the congregation to be greeted personally by Eric, who is regularly seen walking around the church prior to a service, stopping to exchange a few words with each person present. No doubt it is this one-to-one approach, coupled with high standards on the platform, which has contributed substantially to the 'special' Stourbridge atmosphere on which so many have commented over the decades.

Now 86 years old, Eric records here for future generations the story of his beloved church, to which he has selflessly dedicated unlimited time and energy over almost seven decades.

Susan Farrow
London, July 2012

O praise the great eternal mind
In whom all souls are intertwined;
Whose love embraces all mankind,
Whose power pervades creation.
All beings on every shore
Are ruled by His eternal law,
Existing evermore
In constant evolution.

Laura Fisher

Chapter 1

In compiling this history of Stourbridge National Spiritualist Church I am acting upon the wishes of numerous people who have been part of its congregation over the years, and also upon my own desire to see it published whilst my memory is still reasonably good.

At the time of writing, my association with the church has spanned the better part of seventy years but, as I will explain, the Spiritualist community in Stourbridge can trace its roots back to a time well before that.

An extensive report in the local *County Express* speaks of the first church being dedicated in 1926, but my research shows that from the very early 1900s a group of like-minded friends were meeting together in private houses to discuss the philosophy of Spiritualism and practise the phenomena of mediumship.

The first official meeting room, or church, was known as the Gospel Hall, and was in Union Street, Stourbridge. It was initially occupied by the members on a hired basis. Each month the church treasurer James Foxhall and his daughter would make the journey to Norton Stourbridge to deliver the rent to a Mr Perrins, the owner of the freehold.

The premises were dedicated in June, 1926, and it is clear from the *County Express* report that members were keen to share very publicly their pride and pleasure in establishing Stourbridge's first Spiritualist church:

The report records that "the first verse of a hymn was sung outside the building by the congregation, who then filed into the premises, continuing the hymn to the end."

The original Stourbridge Spiritualist Church, formerly known as the Gospel Hall.

The dedication was conducted by B.P. Membery, president of the Midland District Council of the Spiritualists' National Union, who told members that now they had a church of their own, the orthodox churches would be "watching to see what they were going to do." The new church, he said, would "bring to man the certain knowledge that death did not end all, but that he continued in the same personality in the new sphere in which he would find himself after the change called death."

The *County Express* also recorded that Mr Frank A. Smith, who presided over the ceremony, had encouraged the congregation to "unite in a spirit of true brotherly love, and show the world, and Stourbridge in particular, that the service they had undertaken was a service in very truth; that the work would be pioneer work of love and service to their fellow countrymen, and that they would show that, however new Spiritualism appeared to be, it was yet as old as creation."

The speaker and demonstrator on that special day was J.H. Taylor, a respected medium from Walsall. He spoke of the need for members to dedicate their "whole service and energy to the glory of God." The *County Express* reported that Mr Taylor had told the congregation "love was the most essential thing in the life of a church. Often fear and discouragement were found in the minds of members of churches, and that created an unnecessary feeling of jealousy in the hearts of people. In starting that new phase in the life of their church, they should see that they fostered in their hearts the spirit of love. A church became one great family and, with the exercise of the spirit of fellowship and encouragement, that church would grow to great and better things, until those four walls would be too small to hold all the members and the available space around would not be large enough to erect such a building as would be necessary." Mr Taylor's closing words about the size of the building were to prove true in a shorter time than anyone present on that day might have expected.

It is not known how funds were raised to purchase the Gospel Hall as a permanent home for Spiritualism in Stourbridge, but, since no bank would at that time grant a mortgage to a Spiritualist body, one can only assume that the members' dream of owning their own church was fulfilled by a great deal of hard work and fund-raising.

Eric and Mary (Mickey) Wright, stalwarts of the early church.

It seems that by 1936 sufficient money had been raised for a deposit. Accordingly, the church president Eric Wright and his wife Mary (known as 'Mickey'), accompanied by two other church members, travelled to the office of the Spiritualists' National Union in Tib Lane, Manchester, to ask whether the Union's Building Fund Pool would advance a mortgage against the sum that had been raised. The Building Fund Pool had been created to assist Spiritualist churches to acquire or improve premises in the absence of funding from mainstream financial bodies. The visit was successful, and the Gospel Hall, its neighbouring property

Prospect House and land at the back of both buildings were purchased for the sum of £900. Spiritualism in Stourbridge owned a permanent home at last, and though now much extended and improved, that home still stands on the same site today.

****

The Gospel Hall had previously been occupied by the Plymouth Brethren, a strict evangelical Christian movement which took the Bible to be the literal word of God. The building was situated behind a walled garden, approached through a gate. Two steps led up to the entrance, and, climbing them, one was immediately inside the church – there was no vestibule or foyer.

I first visited the church in 1947 and recall that the entrance was quite colourful, with bright linoleum flooring in pale blue. Up the centre aisle, running between the chairs on either side, was a cheerful-looking purple carpet which extended all the way up to the rostrum at the other end of the room. The entrance doorway was also covered with purple carpet so that in times of cold or windy weather the draught could be kept out.

A small carpet runner lay on the floor and was frequently pushed against the door to stop the cold air drifting in from underneath. There was a rudimentary heating system consisting of a series of pipes fixed to the walls, but it was far from adequate and these small efforts at insulation did much for our comfort in those days.

On the left-hand side of the church was a small American harmonium which, in my early days, was played by a Mr Smith. He wasn't always present, and in his absence the instrument was sometimes played by a lady called Audrey Wyatt. On other occasions we would have no musician at all, and at such times we sang our hymns unaccompanied, perhaps with extra gusto to make up for the lack of the harmonium.

On the right-hand side was a curtained-off area behind which the medium or speaker of the day would sit to compose him- or herself before the start of the service. This private area was small, to say the least. Space was at a premium and there was a need to leave as much room as possible to accommodate the growing congregation. At the appointed time the speaker would ascend the couple of steps leading to the rostrum and the service would get under way.

Ernest Oaten,
editor of Two Worlds.
SNU president 1915-1920
and 1922-1923.

It was in this modest building that I was privileged to listen to many dedicated and learned speakers, and to witness some fine demonstrations of mediumship. Luminaries of the Spiritualist movement such as *Two Worlds* editor Ernest Oaten came to lecture, as did the lawyer Harold Vigurs, an outstanding speaker

Harold Vigurs LLB
SNU president 1943-1948.

who was president of the SNU from 1943 to 1948. Harold visited the church on a number of occasions and was a popular and inspiring orator, and a most sincere gentleman. His addresses opened my mind to countless possibilities, and continued to do so until his passing in 1970.

Among others I remember most vividly was a lady named Vi Shakespeare – a capable speaker and a very fine demonstrator of mediumship.

There was also a young fellow named Gordon Higginson who had come out of the army just a year or two earlier. He was outstanding. On the first occasion I heard him, my mother and sister were with me and we all agreed that the survival evidence he conveyed was absolutely phenomenal.

Medium Sally Ferguson

Other fine and memorable exponents of Spiritualism included George Pilkington from Macclesfield, Margaret Webb, Minister Albert Taylor, Bristol-based medium and speaker Sidney Crocker, Arthur Whyman, Joseph Capstack and Sally Ferguson, who would later become a great friend.

In those early days there were several people who were prominent in the church community. One man I well remember was the secretary when I first visited the church – his name was Albert Jones. Unfortunately, no photograph of Albert has survived, but he had a distinctive white moustache and looked like a very benevolent gentleman, which indeed he was. As a result he was known to the congregation as 'Father' Jones. He was a lovely man, held in great esteem by all.

Jim Foxhall, the treasurer, could be a little dour at times, but he took his job very seriously and was absolutely determined to keep the books in order. Everything had to be accounted for and he would never allow a single penny to go astray. His fellow committee members were similarly dedicated, since they considered it a privilege and something of an achievement to belong to the committee of such a vibrant and expanding church.

Chapter 2

In the years following its dedication, the church grew and thrived. The members' delight in owning their own premises was palpable and inspired them with even greater enthusiasm to encourage ever-increasing numbers of people to experience what a Spiritualist church could offer.

Eventually, it became clear that the building was inadequate to cater for the sheer number of folk who attended public meetings or divine services. It could comfortably accommodate only eighty people, and space was needed for many more.

Alongside the regular services, a range of other activities flourished, aimed not only at strengthening the community of Spiritualists but also at raising funds for a future extension to the church premises. Quiz nights, whist-drives, parties and concerts were held, and slowly but surely the dream of a larger space drew closer to becoming a reality. And all the while, wonderful phenomena were experienced by those who were privileged to be crowded inside the building.

****

Early in my association with the church I learned that Mickey and Eric Wright, both of whom had contributed so much to its establishment, opened their house and grounds at Worcester Road, Clent, for an annual summer garden party. The large garden in front of their home, Low Cottage, was approached via a long driveway and behind the house was another substantial garden. Each year it was decorated in festive style with bright awnings, tables and stalls.

After the first year or two, the party became so popular that

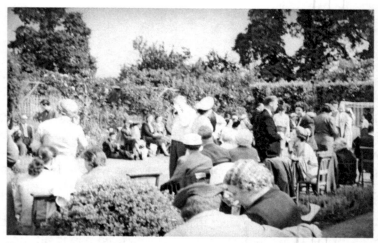

A scene from one of the many successful church garden parties hosted by Mickey and Eric Wright.

we had to hire a Midland Red coach to transport those without cars from Stourbridge. There was a further reason for the coach: public transport was less than frequent and would also have been inconvenient or inaccessible for some people. In addition, people from Wolverhampton church, who had heard about the parties, came to join us. I particularly recall that Florrie and Charles George, who were prominent in the Wolverhampton church at that time, always made the party their summertime 'Mecca'.

Richard Ellidge, SNU General Secretary 1947-1976.

Over the years, Mickey and Eric went to great lengths to ensure the success of those garden parties. Mickey cooked and made lots of advance preparations, stockpiling cakes and other food so that we had an abundance on the day. But she wasn't alone in her efforts, because other members of the church baked cakes, pies and so on. Of course, we had all kinds of stalls where people could buy items or play traditional games such as throwing balls into a bucket, spinning the wheel, hoopla, egg and spoon races, and all manner of other things. The parties were lovely, cheerful events and people went home afterwards full of the joys of spring and full of the delicious produce that had been served to them.

We often invited special guests to the garden parties, including Richard Ellidge, Harry Dawson and Joseph Capstack, all luminaries of the SNU. One year, Mickey wasn't too well, so Hilda and Bill Perry,

Joseph Capstack,
SNU vice-president.

stalwarts of the church, offered to host the party at their home in Kinver. There was a very large field in front of their house, though we could use only a part of it, and surrounding the house were other smaller areas of garden and lawn. I remember that party very well because Tom and Mabel Hibbs, stalwarts of Spiritualism in Wales and at a national level, came to join us as special guests and opened the event for us.

Leading Welsh Spiritualists, Tom and Mabel Hibbs.

Tom had a great sense of humour, and when people asked if he was a medium, he jokingly answered that he was. Taking him seriously, they pressed him to go into the tent to give some private readings. Apparently, and to his own astonishment, he was pretty good, so much so that when he finished he went to his wife Mabel and said that he was "frightened to death!" Poor Tom had been scared by the accuracy of the things he was saying to the lady sitter, who afterwards declared him "awesome!"

Following Hilda and Bill's garden parties, we held similar events at the home of Gwen and Hartley Jones, in Hagley, and of Sylvia and Charles Gwynn. All of this was to supplement the church activities during the summer months.

****

The King Edward VI Grammar School in Stourbridge.

As a church community we were naturally keen to acquaint the wider public with all that Spiritualism had to offer. To that end we organised a number of propaganda meetings in public venues, two of which took place at the King Edward VI Grammar School in Stourbridge. The first, on 26th February 1949, featured a brilliant demonstration of mediumship by a young Gordon Higginson, who was already beginning to make a name for himself as an outstanding exponent.

Extracts from the extraordinary survival evidence given in the demonstration were reported in the weekly Spiritualist newspaper, *Psychic News:*

Gordon Higginson
as a young man.

Gun Borer's Full Name and Address

Brilliant clairvoyance which included many full names and addresses, was given by Mr Gordon Higginson when the Stourbridge National Spiritualist Church held a propaganda meeting in the King Edward VI Grammar School recently.

Addressing a man seated at the back of the hall, Higginson asked: "Do you know the name, Tom Yates?" And, after receiving a positive reply, added, "Are you Tom Yates?"

"Yes," was the reply.

Saying that the recipient's father was communicating, the medium then asked if the address, 11 New Buildings, Price Street, Birmingham, conveyed anything.

The man replied that it did.

That the recipient's mother had passed recently, and references to someone having married twice (the recipient himself) and to a "gun borer" were other references which received verification.

"I am a sporting-gun borer. It is all correct information," was the recipient's comment.

Alfred Wooldridge, a young sergeant air-gunner who lost his life whilst flying over Berlin, was another spirit who gave excellent proof of his survival.

After saying that the above details were correct, the recipient of the message explained the medium's reference to "Caledonia" by saying that the boy's mother lived there.

"He says his wife's name is Wyn and his little girl is Janet," Higginson asserted.

The recipient could not verify the names, but Higginson made fresh contacts and the names were finally corroborated.

Just over a year later, in April 1950, we organised a second successful public event at the Grammar School. A brief article in the local press recorded:

Psychic research had proved of vital importance for it revealed the truth of survival, thereby opening up wide fields of new thought on religion.

This was the view of A.H.L. Vigurs, when he spoke during a meeting held at the Assembly Hall, King Edward VI's Grammar School. This new thought could also be applied to logic and science, averred Vigurs.

Gordon Higginson, the Longton medium, gave a demonstration of clairvoyance. The deputy mayor of Stourbridge presided.

****

Outside the church, a small area ran between the left-hand side of the building and the next-door property, Prospect House. To the right was a small piece of land belonging to the church, on which stood a toilet enclosed in a small brick structure with a wooden door. It was basic in the extreme, having no water supply, and was therefore emptied from time to time by night-soil men. This rather primitive arrangement caused much concern to Percy Brown, a retired senior clerk, who had become president during the

Percy Brown, church president 1940-1959.

war years when Eric Wright had enlisted in the RAF. Percy was greatly embarrassed that visiting lady mediums had to use such a basic facility. He vowed that if he could fulfil just one wish before he died, it would be to have that toilet removed and replaced with a more sophisticated version.

Behind the church was a large area of land, accessed via a pathway on the left-hand side of the building. Unfortunately this area was landlocked because a wall on its right-hand side shut it off completely, and the properties next to it were owned by other people.

By 1951 it had become apparent that the Gospel Hall was of insufficient size to accommodate the increasing number of people attending the weekly divine service. There was space for only eighty to sit, but many more were keen to attend. There were also other issues to be addressed. The only facility for making tea and coffee required a precipitous descent into the cellar by means of a flight of steps outside the building, and of course there was Percy Brown's determination that proper toilet and wash-basin facilities for men and women should be installed within the church building.

The newly extended Stourbridge
National Spiritualist Church.

The difficulty was that after the war restrictions were imposed on many of the raw materials involved in building. Permits had to be obtained for all materials and permission was required for the extension of any existing premises. Eventually we were successful in getting plans approved for an extension to the left-hand side of the church. Thus the main entrance was moved from the front to the left-hand side of the building, and on either side of that entrance ladies' and gents' toilets were installed. No longer would visiting mediums have to endure the formerly primitive facilities. Percy Brown's long-held wish had become a reality.

We also took the opportunity to clear the front garden, so that the garden wall could be demolished to create a car park at the front of the church building. At the same time, we extended the car park in front of Prospect House, the next-door property which we owned.

Because of the extension to the church we were also able to

install a separate kitchen behind the ladies' toilet. It had new brick-built walls, window and skylight, a door leading to the outside and another leading into the church itself. We were extremely proud of that kitchen, although it was modest by today's standards, with not much more than a sink, a small gas stove, some crockery cupboards and a cutlery drawer. Nevertheless, many memorable meals were cooked there and one in particular stands out in my memory, not least because it was served to 80 people.

Chapter 3

Such was the enthusiasm of the small social committee for our newly enlarged premises that they decided to hold a church dinner. This might have been considered overly optimistic given the size of the kitchen, but they were completely undeterred and set about building a temporary extension from the side of the kitchen to the wall of the house next door. It was built with 'Handy Angle' (a construction system consisting of metal uprights bolted together) which we covered with thick polythene. I recall that we were particularly grateful for the polythene that night, since the rain was coming down in torrents!

Under the shelter of this home-made extension we used Calor Gas stoves to supplement the gas stove in the kitchen, resulting in the need for some distinctly unorthodox cooking methods. I'm sure that health and safety people would have had something to say about it nowadays, but things were different then and we happily dropped potatoes, cabbage, peas and so on into metal buckets and let them bubble away on top of those portable stoves. Once cooked, they were served with the turkey that had been roasting in the kitchen and, amid much merriment and camaraderie, all 80 diners enjoyed a meal fit for a king. The problems we encountered in cooking the food were of no consequence because we were a joyous lot. Needless to say, when it was all over, the committee members were absolutely worn out.

Though scores of meals have been served at the church since those days, from kitchens far better equipped, I doubt whether any has been more thoroughly enjoyed than on that very first occasion in 1952. It was a symbol of our growing success as a church community – another milestone for Spiritualism in Stourbridge.

The kitchen and toilets were not the only new additions to our building. Behind the kitchen we now had a dual-purpose room, reached by climbing a couple of steps onto the newly extended church rostrum, then taking a couple of steps down the other side. It was known as the anteroom, and mediums would wait quietly there before services until such time as they approached the platform through the connecting door to deliver their address or demonstrate. Though the room was not large we also used it for committee meetings, because there were only about eight committee members in those days. The rostrum had been fashioned out of a newly created area in order to free up an additional fifteen or so seats in the main body of the church. We managed with those extra facilities until 1976 when, as I shall explain later, a further extension was built.

Needless to say, we were eager to give the local community an opportunity to find out more about our beliefs, and in 1953 we organised a public meeting in Stourbridge Town Hall, at which the great healer Harry Edwards agreed to demonstrate his work. The event was advertised in the local press and the hall was absolutely packed for the wonderful demonstration by Harry and his colleagues George and Olive Burton. The event was subsequently reported in the *County Express*.

Derek Westlake

After the demonstration, the church president Percy Brown invited Harry Edwards and the Burtons to have supper at the home he shared with his companion Derek Westlake, and I was privileged to join them. We were served an excellent meal and had a wonderful evening.

*Famous healer Harry Edwards, who demonstrated his work at
a propaganda meeting in Stourbridge Town Hall in 1953.*

George and Olive Burton, colleagues of Harry Edwards.

Whilst we were very fortunate to have the company of Harry and his entourage, I'm inclined to think that they in turn were delighted by Percy and Derek's hospitality. Late that night, the Burtons insisted on driving Harry back to his healing sanctuary at Burrows Lea in Surrey, a distance of more than 150 miles, and without the luxury of the motorways that cross the country today. I can only imagine they must all have been very tired by the time they arrived home.

Healing has always played a prominent part in the life of our church. In the early days, those who had a healing gift would dispense it at the conclusion of a service, or sometimes at the open circle which was held on Wednesdays.

Later, it was felt that healing needed to have special status within the church, so regular Thursday evening sessions were instituted. They were always under the supervision of an experienced healing leader, who made sure that nothing untoward took place in the conduct of healing, and also gave guidance and instruction to new trainees.

Over the years, many healers have given their time and dedication to help those in need, across a very wide range of maladies. Each and every one of them is worthy of mention and I have appended a complete list of names in an appendix at the back of this book.

****

In 1957 we organised another event at the Town Hall, at which Harold Vigurs gave a talk about what Spiritualism stood for, and explained some of its philosophy. Gordon Higginson shared the platform with him and gave an excellent demonstration of mediumship. As with the previous event, it was advertised locally and the hall was packed.

The church had been registered for marriages in 1947 and had its own 'authorised person', meaning that weddings could

28

Minister Albert Taylor

take place without the need for the local registrar to be present. Minister Albert Taylor, from Birmingham, was the first authorised person and he would come to Stourbridge whenever he was needed.

The first recorded wedding in the church took place in 1948 and was that of James Foxhall (the treasurer I have already mentioned) and his bride Gladys Lewis. That was followed in 1955 by my own marriage to Heather Jermy. In 1973 I succeeded Albert Taylor as authorised person and was joined in that role a few years later by Harry Saich. As I write in 2012, he has only recently retired from the post, which has been taken on by Laraine Killarney and Kath Garrad. To date, 62 weddings have taken place at the church.

On 12th June 1958 the church entered into sole trust with the Spiritualists' National Union, following a unanimous decision by church members. In the case of a sole trust all property belonging to the church is vested under a trust deed with the Union as sole trustees.

All personal property and monies of the church not vested under this deed are vested in the officers and committee in trust for the church. In the case of such a trust the Union appoints two wardens – a Panel (national) Warden and a Local Warden – to act for it in connection with management of the trust property. At the time of writing I am the former and Michael Rumble is the latter.

Throughout the 1960s the church community continued to grow and thrive, with many fine mediums and speakers conducting the services. We also enjoyed further dinner parties, for one of which, in 1967, members paid 7s 6d. At a subsequent dinner the cost was

12s 6d, and by 1970 the cost for attending our sixth dinner party was 15s 6d. There was no doubt the cost of living was rising!

Throughout the 1950s and 60s we ran a vibrant weekly discussion class, led by Percy Brown. The level of debate was very high and attracted some prominent attendees from other religious groups in the area. Mr and Mrs Manny Rose came from the Liberal Jewish Synagogue, and the Unitarian minister Alfred Heal and his wife also attended. Mrs Alice Tudor, and Mr and Mrs Biggs, came to us from the local Methodist church.

Unitarians Minister and Mrs Alfred Heal, members of the weekly discussion group.

We always began with the same hymn, deliberately chosen for its non-denominational words about truth, to which all who attended could subscribe without any compromise to their individual beliefs.

The first verse ran:

> *O Truth! Thou art the only way*
> *By which we rise from night to day;*
> *O Truth! Thou refuge of the soul!*
> *When storms of change begin to roll,*
> *When worlds decay, and faiths depart,*
> *Our steadfast resting-place Thou art.*

*Percy Brown enjoys a well-earned rest after his
years of dedicated service to the church.*

The two verses of this hymn were followed by a few moments of
silent meditation, after which the leader would read a passage of a
spiritual or philosophical nature which would form the basis of the
evening's discussion. A very wide range of topics were debated,
from spiritual philosophers and thinkers of many disciplines. I
particularly recall that the words of White Eagle, Silver Birch,
Mahatma Gandhi, other Eastern philosophers, Maurice Barbanell
and other Spiritualist writers gave rise to some interesting
discussion that was at times expressed quite passionately, but
always with courtesy.

When Percy stepped down as president in 1959 he was
succeeeded by Major Vic Mound, and I took over the leadership
of the discussion class. In 1963 I was elected president, and a few
years later Dennis Elwell, a church member and assistant editor
of the local paper, took over the class from me. As a token of our

esteem and graditude for Percy's dedicated service to the church, we presented him with a very comfortable armchair, in which he had certainly earned the right to relax.

****

In November 1966 we had a visit from Melvin Smith, president of the International Spiritualist Federation, who came to take a service. It was reported in the local *County Express* and also in *Psychic News*.

This is what PN wrote:

"Spiritualism is the most misunderstood philosophy in the world." So said Melvin Smith, International Spiritualist Federation president, during his first visit to the Midlands.

Melvin Smith, president of the International Spiritualist Federation during the 1960s.

Reporting the meeting he took at Stourbridge Spiritualist Church, Worcs., the 'County Express' quoted him as saying:

"People think we meet in the dark, and that there are floating tables and voices out of the air. They believe that all we want is to talk to the spirits of the dead, and that our preoccupation is with the next life.

"But Spiritualism is a philosophy of living for us here and now. We believe that this moment of our life is the most important. We believe that if we live well now the next life will take care of itself."

The newspaper, in its excellent account, commented on Smith's demonstration of clairvoyance:

"Connoisseurs of this kind of demonstration were able to compare the American method with that more usual among English mediums. While the English demonstrator will often spend several minutes on the one 'message' in an attempt to make it as evidential as possible, his American counterpart has a less laboured approach and speaks to more people for less time. Rather than relying on details like names and addresses he trusts that the 'message' will carry its own conviction."

Chapter 4

*The footpath to Enville Common, one of the main locations
for the church's summer treasure-hunt.*

In May 1970 my family and I moved to a house in Broughton
Road, Stourbridge. Since it had a rather larger garden than our
previous home, we decided in 1972 to host a church garden party
ourselves. It was very successful, so much so that we were asked
if we would hold another one. We agreed with pleasure, all tickets
were quickly sold and people greatly looked forward to the event.

It being mid-summer, we anticipated fine weather and had set
out an array of tables and chairs, colourful stalls and games in the
garden. Entertainers had been booked and people arrived dressed
in summer clothes. Imagine our dismay when the heavens opened,
rain came down in torrents and everything we had set up outside
was virtually washed away.

Determined that the unpredictable British weather would not spoil our day, we all made a dash for shelter in the house. People sat on the stairs, in the extensions, in the lounge, the kitchen and the conservatory, and even at tables in the garage. The entertainers agreed to give their performance twice so that everyone would be able to enjoy it. They stood at the far end of the lounge, and at the end of the show the first audience gave way to the second and the whole thing was repeated. It was certainly an unorthodox garden party, but no less enjoyable for all that. Indeed, many people remarked afterwards that they had enjoyed it at least as much as the previous one, which was held in bright sunshine.

****

In 1972 we decided to start a magazine for church members. Entitled *Link*, it was edited jointly by Albert Buckley and Cissie Shaw, and contained news of church events alongside news of individuals in our community. There were also philosophical articles, personal experiences, poems and humorous items, all aimed at keeping members up-to-date with what was happening in the church community. The editorship was later taken over by Julie Waters and Joyce Sharples,

with assistance from Mary Barratt, Dorothy Marshall, Toni and Frank McGrann and June Hughes.

In the summer of that year we held a treasure-hunt with a difference. It had been organised by our social committee, and the treasure was to be hunted by car. On a sunny Sunday evening we finished the service by 7.45 and made an immediate dash for our vehicles. The hunt was on!

The clues were unusual and we had already been given the first, which would lead us to a location somewhere in the countryside between Stourbridge and Staffordshire. Once there, we would discover the next clue, and so on, until the final location, near Arley, was reached and the treasure found. To the best of my recollection it was a large box of chocolates. When the hunt was over we adjourned, tired but very cheerful, to a nearby hostelry.

Prior to the starting of the magazine, the number of people attending the church had risen to a point where we needed to think about extending the building for a second time. In addition, we had not been utilising the land behind the church, which had deteriorated to a rugged state and was overgrown with long grass and weeds. It was a waste of valuable space and the time had come to do something with it. We began to consider what type of extension we might build, and of course to start the long process of raising the considerable funds needed to pay for it.

In 1972, as we were in the early stages of planning, a proposal was put forward by the local authority in Dudley to pull down the houses on the right-hand side of the church building, and also to demolish a nearby public house, to which in previous years many church members had adjourned for a drink after the evening service. All these properties were deemed beyond repair and the proposal was to replace them with flats for senior citizens, thereby cramming a lot more accommodation into the available space. In consequence of that, plans were submitted to the relevant council department for approval.

As luck would have it, Dennis Elwell happened to be present at the council meeting when this proposal came up for discussion. He was concerned about the fact that the planned new homes were going to occupy all the land next door to the church, and also that a road would be created at the bottom end of this plot of land. This meant, in effect, that our piece of land behind the church (which was already landlocked) would still be landlocked and therefore virtually useless to us.

Having been made aware of this by Dennis, I made representations to the local authority but by and large they fell on deaf ears. However, luck was with us again since we had a church committee member who was an education officer for the same local authority. His name was Albert Buckley and he was very dedicated to the church. He therefore used his influence on colleagues who

were involved in the planning and building departments, and prevailed upon them to meet with me.

So it was that Albert, the church secretary Cissie Shaw and I met with three local authority representatives, and in consequence they recommended that the plans for the new road should be reconsidered. It was then proposed that rather than being at the lower end of the street, the new road would be immediately adjacent to the church and would feed the flats.

Cissie Shaw, who has served the church in many capacities.

And this was exactly what came about. I should record here my thanks to a gentleman named Ron Skelton who was a colleague of Albert Buckley. Ron was in charge of planning and persuaded the local authority to change their plans so that we could have a narrow road directly alongside the church, leading out into Union Street.

We were told, however, that when the road was constructed we would have to pay half its cost. In addition, we would have to supply half its maintenance charges in perpetuity. We would also have to fund the cost of a wall that would separate the church from the adjacent new properties so that the pathway between would allow us to go right to the back of the land we owned. The road would then facilitate our having an entrance to our landlocked area. That land would later be developed and made into a car park, which was to prove most useful to us.

We held all kinds of small events in the community to raise funds for our intended extension. Amongst them was a horse show which took place on at Penn Orchard Farm in Hagley Wood Lane, Clent. The show was the brainchild of Joyce Bates, and a number of people brought their own horses, horse-boxes and so on. Though we attracted a fair crowd of people we raised only a small amount of money towards the church extension.

The greatest fundraiser by far was the 'buy a brick' scheme, in which people funded the cost of one or more of the bricks which would form the new building. A further marvellous source of funds were the interest-free loans made to us by church members, who received in return a guarantee that their money would be returned to them at some future time. A year or two later, when we were in a position to pay them back, to their great credit many of them refused to accept it.

Chapter 5

The summer of 1976 saw the culmination of almost two years of planning and hard work, as our second phase of extension and rebuilding reached its conclusion. The work had taken seven months to complete and when it was all over we had a much longer church, with a new kitchen on the left-hand side and a new entrance hall. The toilets and entrance which had previously been on the left-hand side were demolished and the extension went straight up to Prospect House on the left, with a new entrance which once again was at the side of the building. There was also a large entrance area into the church itself, which was still on the right-hand side. A larger committee/mediums' room was once again on the left-hand side. In addition, we were able to accommodate the large grand piano which had replaced our previous instrument.

The building of the extension necessarily caused a lot of disruption to the church premises and for a time it was impossible for us to hold our regular services. We were concerned that our congregation might dwindle during the period of closure so we approached the local Unitarian church, in Lower High Street, Stourbridge, to ask if they would allow us to use their building for our Sunday evening divine service. I knew their secretary, Mrs Brown, and she agreed to discuss the possibility with the church elders and trustees who readily agreed that we could use their premises until our building extension was completed.

They generously placed no restrictions whatsoever on the philosophy or demonstrations of mediumship that were to take place. Minister Margaret Pratt, an SNU minister from Scotland, took the first service in the Unitarian church, and very proud we were that night. On each occasion we met there we had the pleasure of the Unitarians' own organist playing their very splendid pipe organ for us. I know from personal experience just how fine it

The Unitarian church in Lower High Street, Stourbridge, which made us so welcome while our building work was carried out.

was, because I subsequently sang to its accompaniment on several occasions during the Unitarians' Sunday morning services.

When we were able to return to our own premises, we not only thanked the Unitarian trustees verbally, we also wrote to them and asked how much we owed for the use of their premises. To their great credit they told us we didn't owe a penny, adding that they were delighted to have provided us with the means to hold our services while the work on our own church was carried out.

Though our newly extended building was almost complete, there were a few finishing touches still to come, not least the construction of a new floor leading from the main entrance to the inside of the new church. This in itself was not a major problem – save for the fact that there was a wedding imminently about to take place.

Graham Dann and his fiancée Jean Morris were members of the church and were greatly looking forward to celebrating their marriage in the newly enlarged building. Though we offered them the chance to make other arrangements because of the unfinished floor, they were adamant that they wanted to go ahead as planned, particularly since a number of their relatives and friends had already arranged to travel some considerable distance for the big day.

So it was that on 4th June 1976, the groom and approximately fifty guests made a most unconventional entrance into the church to await the arrival of the bride – via a series of slightly wobbly wooden planks placed side by side to form a floor.

Jean, clad in a traditional summer wedding dress, arrived with her father a short time later, and negotiated the temporary floor without incident, despite her long dress. Of course, all wedding days are unique, but there can be few brides who have had to walk the plank in order to say "I do!"

The new church building was formally dedicated on 21st August 1976 and part of that dedication was of a beautiful stained-glass window which had been specially designed and made by William Pardoe of Lye. Prior to commissioning the window, Cissie Shaw and I had visited Mr Pardoe on behalf of the church, having heard from others about his skill.

After we had presented our case to him, he told us that he didn't feel able to take on the project because he was growing old and wasn't sure whether he could carry out any new commissions. Perhaps we persuaded him quite strongly, but as we were leaving he agreed to give our request some serious thought and invited us to return in a week to see if he had arrived at a decision. We did so, and to our great delight he agreed to make a window for us. To this day it brings so much pleasure to our congregation and to those who visit the church for funerals, weddings and other special services.

In Mr Pardoe's own words:

The main design of the window consists of a representation of the sun, the emblem of of the Spiritualists' Movement, at the centre, surrounded by a wide border of colour in the form of a vortex; this is based upon a medieval idea of showing the path of life in colour.

Green, the colour of Hope and Spingtime, rises from the depths and portrays young life in its upward striving to attain the Gold of Glory in the centre, while Red, the colour of Adversity, assails and influences us from either side. It blends with the green in its upward struggle and finally emerges and disappears into the Blue of the Eternal at the apex of the window.

We also placed a new painting in the church, done by Jean Sisley, a member of our congregation. She was a very competent artist and her interpretation of Albrecht Dürer's famous 'Praying Hands' still hangs in the church today.

Among our special guests for that memorable service of dedication was *Psychic News* editor Maurice Barbanell, who a few days later published an article about his visit to Stourbridge. The following is his account of that special day:

Mayor pays tribute at church's rededication

To attend last Saturday's rededication service at Stourbridge National Spiritualist Church, W. Midlands, following its extension, meant a round journey by car of 300 miles and took eleven hours but it was a rewarding experience.

It was just over half a century earlier that local Spiritualists acquired what was then a gospel hall used by the Plymouth Brethren.

The date for this service had been postponed because Councillor Dennis Harty, Mayor of Dudley wanted to be present with his wife, the lady mayoress.

The rededication was done by SNU president Gordon Higginson. He recalled that his first meeting in that church was over forty years ago, when he was fourteen. Gordon congratulated them on the magnificent

Maurice and Sylvia Barbanell

transformation which doubles the church's accommodation.

'Spiritualism is not a branch of any other religion.' he stressed. Its profound message was 'We are all gods in the making.'

The mayor unveiled a beautiful stained glass window depicting the sun. It is the work of William Pardoe, a splendid craftsman, who presented it to the church.

The mayor thought it 'a fine thing these days for any church to increase its membership.'

Church president Eric Hatton told the heart-warming, behind the scenes story leading to their accomplished task. Modestly, he said nothing about his own contribution, praising his enthusiastic, dedicated and hard-working committee and members as being responsible for it.

He, however, was the driving force for this new church when it was decided to rebuild on its site two years ago. One member told me, 'We would do anything for our president.'

Much of the strenuous work involved was of the do-it-yourself kind. As one example, Eric mentioned they had to move 1,200 tons of earth!

43

The money for the extension was raised by a variety of methods – coffee mornings, bring and buy sales, bazaars offering nearly new objects, with enough of these still stored for at least another dozen similar functions. Finally an advance from the SNU building fund pool enabled the project to get under way.

James Foxhall, treasurer in the early days of the church.

Eric praised the local authority's co-operation. They agreed to construct a new road to the car park behind the church and made no charge for doing so, or for its maintenance.

He paid tribute to the local Unitarian church, whose minister was present, for accommodating them during the time when they could not meet.

*Percy Wilson, M.A.
SNU president 1950-1953.*

Eric invited the oldest member of his church, James Foxhall, whose 81ˢᵗ birthday was the previous Sunday, to address the audience. Then he asked someone even older, Percy Wilson, who is 83 to speak. Percy, looking a little frail but very game, had come with his wife Winifred all the way from Oxford to be there.

Percy presented to the church its excellent amplification system. This provided opportunities, amongst other things, for recordings of classical music to be played.

In a firm voice, Percy said: "I come to give you greetings from our pioneers." He mentioned the fact, of which he was rightly proud, that he was dedicated to Spiritualism when only six weeks old. In the intervening period he had rededicated himself more than once!

When I, too, was asked to speak, I explained to the mayor and his wife the reason for the sunflower being chosen as a symbol in a badge many Spiritualists wear. It always turns its face to the sun.

I pointed out that it was not so very long ago that Spiritualists were 'rogues and vagabonds'. Our successful campaign to change antiquated laws, which denied us religious and legal freedom, had made us respectable, as shown by the presence of the mayor and mayoress. We still, however, had to reach the stage where we were respected.

Evidence of the splendid co-operation existing among the committee was the fact that a lavish tea was served, free of

The newly extended church, photographed from the rostrum.

charge, to every one of the 200 people present. I pay tribute to these Midlands Spiritualists who are part of the backbone of our movement. They work unremittingly without thought of limelight or publicity. Throughout Britain their story can be duplicated many times.

My journey to Stourbridge took much longer than the one returning to London. I lost my way more than once. Even when Stourbridge was reached, I was misdirected. When I stopped to ask the way, my wife and I saw a genial middle-aged couple approaching. 'They look as if they are Spiritualists,' said my wife. She was right, and they were on their way to the church. So, by giving them a lift, we were able to arrive about fifteen minutes before the service began.

Clearly, Maurice Barbanell had enjoyed our special service of rededication, but he could not have enjoyed it any more than we did. It marked the fulfilment of a dream – not just my dream, but the dream of all the many church members who had worked with such commitment to make it a reality.

I should mention that although the wall was built, the workmen used various expletives while completing it, and one said to me that he didn't know what b****y influence I'd got, but that wall would have cost many, many thousands of pounds to erect and they had been pushed on because the mayor was dedicating it on a Saturday very soon and their lives would probably be in peril if it wasn't finished in time! Since then we have never paid a penny for the road and its upkeep, or for the wall. We are still greatly indebted to the local authority for that concession. And to the mayor for his ability to terrorise the workforce!

Chapter 6

From the autumn of 1976 our newly extended premises were put to full and enthusiastic use as we held numerous events including many joyous concerts and musical evenings, with local singers and musicians as well as those from further afield. At one point we even brought a full-sized bowling alley into the church and spent an evening in friendly (if rather noisy) competition!

We also arranged a number of outside events such as a trip to the theatre to see the much-publicised musical, *Hair*, a visit to a medicinal herb garden and a boat trip along the local canal, during which we shared a traditional meal of fish and chips.

Themed social events were very popular with our members, and one was a memorable Hawaiian evening. Guests were transported to a tropical paradise as they arrived to find the room bedecked with real palm trees. Hawaiian guitar music played softly in the background as people relaxed on chairs decorated with palm leaves. Tables were laid with brightly coloured cloths and other Hawaiian-style adornments, while the food was also typically Hawaiian. I recall that we enjoyed an excellent meal in which pineapple featured prominently!

Staying with the culinary theme, we also hosted a 'rich-man, poor-man' meal, through which we raised a good deal of money for children in Africa. The idea was that two types of meal were prepared and when members arrived they each chose a sealed envelope that contained a slip of paper indicating which type of meal they would be served. Though the poor man's meal was much simpler than the rich man's, it was nonetheless filling and tasty, and was enjoyed by all who ate it. On another occasion we hosted a harvest supper with a good three-course meal for 53 people, and many other harvest meals followed over the years.

We also made a decision to become involved with the Council of Faiths, an organisation dedicated to promoting knowledge and mutual understanding between members of different religions and denominations. The decision had come about because of my friendship with George Cloak, a Methodist I had met when singing at one of their services in Pensnett, Brierley Hill. George was already involved with the C of F and encouraged me to join.

So it was that Stourbridge Spiritualists, represented by Cissie Shaw and myself, met with local Anglicans, Hindus, Methodists, Muslims, Roman Catholics, Sikhs and others, gaining a greater understanding of each other's beliefs and forming new friendships in the process.

In consequence of my friendship with a Hindu named Bei Sharma, we extended an invitation to him and fellow members of the Birmingham Hindu community to come to our church and talk to us about Hinduism, and about their work locally and worldwide. Their talk was well attended and much enjoyed, and as a result we decided to arrange a second visit.

This time, to our surprise and delight, our Hindu friends brought two Sikh musicians with them. They entertained us with traditional Sikh music and meditations, explaining the significance of each as they went along.

After their first visit, I asked Bei Sharma if they would stay and have some refreshments with us, but he politely declined, saying that he and his friends ought to return home. This puzzled me, because it was still quite early in the evening. Sharma explained that they would have to get up at about 5.30am and therefore had to go to bed very early. I asked why they had to rise at that time, and he explained that they would normally carry out their ablutions and wash themselves completely before prayers. Afterwards, they would have a small meal before heading off to work. It was quite enlightening. We were very much drawn to our visitors and it was fascinating to learn this new information

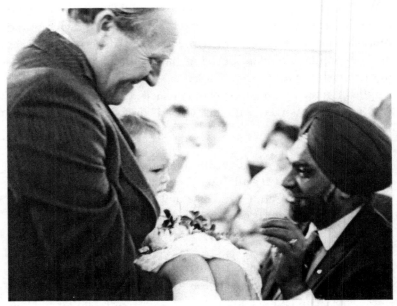

*This naming ceremony provided a joyful example
of inter-faith friendship.*

about their daily lives.

Later, as I conducted a baby's naming ceremony – one of nearly
a hundred to have taken place in our church – I was delighted
to see that a Sikh friend of the child's parents was present and
taking a keen interest in the service. As with the Council of Faiths
it demonstrated the friendship and respect which can develop
between members of different religions.

I also served on the organising committee for One World Week,
which was designed to show how different faith communities
could work successfully together. We held events at the Concert
Hall in Dudley, for which I provided tables and equipment from
my business. Money was raised at these events, but their primary
purpose was to demonstrate that diverse religious communities
could work together for a common goal. I remember becoming
friendly with a gentleman from the Islamic community who was
on that committee. Sadly, I have now lost track of him.

I ordain Mary Duffy as a minister of the SNU.

On 2nd April 1977 I celebrated a significant milestone in my own life as a Spiritualist, when I became the third member of our church to be ordained a minister of the Spiritualists' National Union. Gordon Higginson, who was by then president of the Union, travelled to Stourbridge to conduct the ceremony.

Some years later it was my privilege to conduct an ordination service myself, for the much-loved medium Mary Duffy. Mary was a dear friend to many in the church, and a packed congregation came to witness her special day.

In the late 1970s Mickey Ellis, who had remarried following the passing of her husband Eric Wright, decided to start what became known as the Sunflower Club. It was a flourishing group which met monthly, on a Thursday afternoon, and was intended primarily for church members who had reached retirement age. A collection was taken after each meeting, and a donation made to the church at the end of each year.

Each month a speaker would be invited to give a talk on his or her specialist topic, ensuring that a wide range of subjects would be covered. One such speaker was John Sparry – a book historian and an expert on the history of this area. Another memorable speaker was the well-known singer Cecil Drew, who not only spoke enthrallingly about the world of music, but also treated his audience to some songs.

Homeopathy was covered by Betty King, and massage by the blind masseuse Mrs Holdsworth. Club members Cissie Shaw and Mary Simmonds also spoke about their experiences at a Buddhist camp. Long-time church member Win Brown eventually took over the running of the club from Mickey and continued to lead it until 2005. Win, who by that time was in her late eighties, had been a dedicated leader, but sadly there was no one available to take over from her.

Around that time, a group of us from the church hired a train to take us on a summer evening journey through the stunning scenery of the Severn Valley. I took along a portable cassette player so that we could enjoy some music while the train meandered gently through the countryside. The atmosphere was very jolly, as we moved from carriage to carriage enjoying each other's company and staring out at the beautiful scenery passing by the windows. It was an evening to remember, and I still smile when I recall it.

****

Large demonstrations of mediumship featured prominently during the next few years, with many renowned exponents taking part. At the same time, we continued to provide opportunities for refining the sensitivity and intuition of our own members by means of awareness and development circles. In the early days these were led by various practising mediums, including Mary Wright, Hilda Perry and Heather Hatton. The structured classes which now operate aim to help people understand their psychic sensitivity, and whatever ability they may have in a mediumistic sense.

In addition we hold frequent seminars and workshops covering a

Gordon Higginson MSNU
SNU president 1970-1993.

wide range of subjects. These always prove popular and invariably take place on a Saturday, when a visiting medium from afar has come to Stourbridge to take the whole weekend's services.

In 1979 we were privileged to offer a series of lectures about Spiritualism, given by Gordon Higginson, each of which was so much appreciated by the nearly fifty people who enrolled. Gordon covered a wide range of subjects, beginning with a talk on what Spiritualism stood for. In subsequent lectures he covered the implications of Spiritualism and the responsibility of being a Spiritualist, the phenomena of Spiritualism, and the running of circles.

Prior to the final lecture Gordon agreed that he would end the series with a demonstration of physical mediumship – news which delighted those who would be attending. When the time came, a circle of chairs was arranged around him, and before taking their seats everyone was searched by one of two appointed ladies or gentlemen.

Searches such as these are necessary before a physical séance because it can be dangerous for the medium if unplanned light sources or jewellery with reflective surfaces are brought into the séance room. Gordon himself was searched by members of the church to ensure that he had not concealed anything. I well remember that examination, because an old friend of mine was embarrassed at the prospect of checking Gordon's person.

Heather Hatton received an apported flower during Gordon Higginson's séance.

The searches complete, Gordon took his seat and, after a short time, fell into trance. The séance began in darkness, and his guides spoke to us in both philosophical and jovial terms, each having their own individual way of communicating.

Then we were told that an experiment was about to take place, and a short while later Gordon's guide Choo Chow asked that the red light be turned on. Earlier in the proceedings a number of us had sensed that something was happening with Gordon, and as the red light was switched on we saw that ectoplasm was coming from his mouth. The quantity was not large, but it was nonetheless remarkable, bearing in mind that we had never before sat as a group, and as a result Gordon's guides would have had to work with many unfamiliar energies.

At the end of the proceedings we discovered a fresh flower – a red carnation – in the centre of the circle, its petals still wet with dew. At the suggestion of the guide it was given to Heather, who was thrilled to receive it. However, there was one lady present who longed for the flower and expressed a wish that she could have had something like it. The lady was Kate Pratt, and Heather, out of her generous heart, gave it to her and her son Ron. Overjoyed, Kate put the flower in a book and pressed it, and Ron retained it until his passing on 2nd March 2012.

Ron Pratt held various offices in the church during his many decades of membership.

****

From the late 1970s onwards the church had a group of ladies who were interested in learning about flower arranging. Nora Perkins, an expert flower arranger, was not a member of the church but had a friend who was, and agreed to come along and instruct people in the art of creating floral arrangements.

In 1978 we established a more formal floral group, which is still active today. It was born from a combination of ideas, but Heather Hatton was particularly influential in its commencement. The group began to meet on a weekly basis, and a rota was established to ensure that the important job of providing attractive floral arrangements to adorn the church for Sunday services was shared out among its members.

Floral displays were also provided for special events in the church, such as weddings, funerals and namings. The group had a social element, too, with members meeting for dinner and making visits to places of horticultural interest such as gardens and nurseries. Before long they had become very proficient in the art of flower arrangement and were keen to share their enthusiasm for all things floral with a wider public. They therefore decided to hold a flower festival in the summer of that year, and to open it to the general public, advertising it in the local papers and library.

Entitled 'A Journey into Light', it was to be the first of many such events, and drew a lot of people from outside the Spiritualist community. The festival took place from Saturday 8th to Monday 10th July, during which time wonderful arrangements of flowers graced the church entrance and many passers-by came inside to admire the various displays in the church itself. They began with a floral representation of the sun's golden rays pouring out light, heat, and the essence of God, bringing forth life. The visitor was then led on a journey from birth through learning, courage, torments, devotion and heightened awareness, and finally towards the light, which was represented by a single white lotus blossom in a shallow blue dish, overhung by a white branch symbolising the tree of life. The festival closed on Monday evening with a concert by bass-baritone Harry Millward and soprano Patsy Smith, both very fine singers who were accompanied on the piano by Marjorie Penn.

Shortly afterwards, a group of us spent a very pleasant day at Walsall Arboretum, a beautiful 73-hectare park which first opened to the public in 1874. People enjoyed the visit so much that in the following year we decided to visit the Arboretum in Highley. It specialised in beautiful displays of garden flowers, and also had areas where masses of bluebells and daffodils grew wild, forming a vast sea of colour.

In the summer of 1979 we set off by coach to Weston-super-Mare, intending to enjoy a leisurely afternoon at the seaside. It was a lovely sunny day, and all went according to plan, until we were back on the road and heading for home. All of a sudden the coach came to a juddering halt halfway up a steep hill on the way to Bristol. All attempts by the driver to restart the engine failed dismally, and

The main entrance to Highley Arboretum

there was nothing for it but to get out and push. We all climbed off, rolled up our sleeves, and once the driver had firmly engaged the brake to stop the coach rolling back down the hill, we began to push with all our might in the hope of bump-starting the engine. Alas, our efforts were in vain. The driver contacted an official from the coach company, who agreed to send a replacement vehicle to rescue us. By the time it arrived and took us all the way back to Stourbridge, the dawn was almost coming up. One way and another, it had been a memorable day!

•

Chapter 7

The year 1981 saw the establishment of various new groups, each designed to promote the church in a particular way. It had also been designated 'International Year of Disabled Persons' and the Floral Group decided to hold another festival, from Saturday 4th to Monday 6th July. Once again, the floral displays were excellent, and were specifically created with themes connected to the disabled community.

For the blind there was a strongly scented arrangement of garden flowers. Other themed displays were designed to represent the lame, the mentally handicapped, the deaf, those with heart disease, the age disabled, the young disabled and the speech impaired. There was also a tribute in rainbow colours dedicated to those who devoted their lives to the needs of others, and another depicting the International Year of Disabled Persons' logo.

On the Saturday evening we held a concert with many local artists taking part, and on the Monday there was a special open evening for the disabled.

The *County Express* carried the following report of the festival in their 10th July edition:

Spiritualist Church flower festival

Ladies of the Spiritualist Church in Stourbridge were thinking of the disabled in many ways last week.

Not only were they raising money for them in this the "Year of the Disabled" but they made sure disabled people could enjoy their "Flower Festival".

Floral group members Miss G. Tonks, Mrs M. Ellis,
Mrs M. Simmonds and Mrs M. Edwards
with part of the July 1981 floral display.

The floral displays were arranged to depict many forms of disablement and there was a special scented arrangement for the blind.

Many visitors toured the festival at the Church in Union Street over the weekend. The festivities included a "Grand Concert" performed by many local artists, a Sunday Service and an open evening for the disabled.

The ladies who helped create the displays included: Mrs P Wagstaffe, Miss A Butler, Mrs T Tapling, Mrs C Shaw, Mrs M Ellis, Mrs H Hatton, Mrs G Hubbard and Miss N Perkins. All proceeds from the festival will be donated to local charities for the disabled.

In the same year, we staged an Old Tyme Music Hall, for which Howard Price, a friend of mine from South Wales, came all the way to Stourbridge to act as master of ceremonies. Howard had a great gift for humour and as a result was a brilliant MC. I was friendly with a number of local artists from the Gilbert & Sullivan society and other musical groups, and persuaded them to come along and take part. Howard's wife Mollie was also there. She was a very good impressionist and also read poetry, so she contributed to the event herself. Ron Pratt, a long-standing church member and gifted amateur actor, delivered two monologues, one from the Black Country and one period music hall piece. I also took part, singing *The Flower Song* from the Fair Maid of Perth, and another solo entitled *Josephine*. All in all it was a most successful evening, presented to a crowded church.

****

It was around this time that the need for extra car-parking space at the church became pressing. Attendance had grown steadily and there was no longer sufficient space to accommodate people's cars. Purely by coincidence the house and accompanying land adjacent to Prospect House came onto the market because Mr and Mrs Wall, the couple who lived there, were divorcing.

In consequence I suggested to the church committee that we buy the house and land, so that we could make alterations to the accommodation with a view to converting it into a home for elderly Spiritualists. Unfortunately, one or two of the committee were intransigent and would not agree to go ahead with the idea. In some ways I regretted that, but it's fair to say that it would have involved an awful lot of work. Even so, with the right kind of enthusiasm and dedication it could have been achieved and would have fulfilled an important role.

A few months later we were still trying to find additional car-parking space, so I asked Mr and Mrs Wall whether they would sell a portion of the land that lay behind the house. They agreed, and the consequence was that we fenced off the area and had a slope made, so that although it was only rough ground we were able to park extra cars there. Coupled with our existing parking facility it enabled us to accommodate far more vehicles than most churches can do.

****

Sometime afterwards a group of us travelled by coach to Longton in Staffordshire, an area world famous for its high-quality pottery. It was fascinating to watch the potters at work, and to visit the shops where items of locally manufactured pottery could be purchased. Boarding the coach again after our visit, we were driven the short distance to Longton Spiritualist Church, where we ate the meal our friends had prepared for us and then attended a service in the church.

The close friendship between ourselves and members of Gordon Higginson's church at Longton was long standing. From the 1970s we had jointly hosted Longton, Fenton and Stourbridge weeks at Stansted Hall, and they had gained a considerable following. Each year, 60 or 70 people were privileged to have the services of some of the most outstanding mediums and lecturers of the period. Albert Best, Gordon Higginson, Don Galloway, Doris Collins, Mary Duffy, Sally Ferguson, Ivy Scott, Charles Coulston and Wilfred Watts all took part, with the result that the weeks gained a reputation for excellence in both mediumship and teaching.

Ted Turner, a keen collector of antiques.

Our next major fund-raising event was an auction evening, held in the church. It was organised by the pianist Frank Moore, with the help of Ron Pratt and Ted Turner who were enthusiastic and knowledgeable collectors of antiques, and Terri Taplin, who owned a local antique shop. Various people donated items to the auction, but there was no bric-a-brac and all the pieces were of good quality, including a number of paintings.

I recall that Ted took the role of auctioneer and wielded his gavel with high good humour as people signalled their bids in the traditional way, by raising a hand. A great deal of fun was had by those who attended, and a fair sum of money was raised in the process.

Pianists Frank Moore and Michael Thompson.

We were also very fortunate to receive a generous bequest from Stourbridge resident Mrs Margaret Jones. She and her husband Douglas, who had predeceased her by just four months, had no children and had therefore divided their estate between various causes. A report in the local paper stated that following a small number of personal bequests...

"The residue is to be divided equally among the National Spiritualist Church, Stourbridge; the Methodist Church, New Road, Stourbridge; Kidderminster General Hospital ophthalmic department, the Pain Relief Foundation of Walton Hospital,

Liverpool; Cancer Relief MacMillan Fund; RAF Association; Guide Dogs for the Blind Association; Arthritis and Rheumatism Council and British Heart Foundation."

Over the years, we have been blessed with a number of other bequests, notably from Albert Buckley, Edith Coupland, Lucy Hall, Ron Pratt, Helen Rollason and Alice Tudor.

****

In July that same year we held a very special flower festival from 6th to 8th September to celebrate sixty years of Spiritualism in Stourbridge. Our church was now a far cry from the basic facilities enjoyed by those who had begun its journey back in 1926, and we thought it was important to honour the achievements of the past six decades.

Minister Irene Leedham

As I wrote in an introduction to the festival programme:

"Countless numbers of broken hearts have been repaired by contact from their loved ones in Spirit, and many have found a new zest for living when life had lost its purpose. Yes – this church, and those who over the years have helped make it what it is today, have contributed to the welfare of our society. Let our celebrations be a tribute to all that has been achieved, and may we be wise enough to accept inspired guidance for the establishment of a larger spiritual community."

As before, the many floral displays reflected a particular theme, and appropriately on this occasion that theme was anniversaries. The display adorning our diamond-shaped window bore the verse:

This diamond window represents
Souls travelling round the sun,
To die and waste, yet rise again
And evermore live on.
So in this perfect setting
In white and grey we see
Depicted here, our sixtieth year,
Our Diamond Jubilee.

On the Saturday evening we enjoyed a celebratory Grand Concert given by local artists, and the Sunday evening service was conducted by Irene Leedham, an SNU minister and excellent medium who came from Tamworth. On the following Saturday, 13th September, our jubilee celebrations were rounded off with a superb demonstration of mediumship by Gordon Higginson.

Chapter 8

The 1990s began in some style as we hosted a festive Twelfth Night party on 6th January. It was attended by 78 members who were treated to a feast. French onion soup was followed by roast beef and Yorkshire pudding with a selection of vegetables. Fruit pie and cream rounded off what had been an excellent meal, cooked as always in the church kitchen by members of the social committee. Entertainment was provided by some of our own members, accompanied by the pianist Michael Thompson. They were joined by members of West Bromwich Operatic Society, who performed a selection of songs from the shows. It was a joyous evening, a really happy event.

In July that same year we were entertained by the accordionist Barry Smith and his Bavarian band, kitted out in traditional lederhosen and feathered hats. Barry, of course, had overseen the building of our church extension in 1976 and was kindly donating the band's services to help our building fund. In addition to the excellent music making there was plenty of joking and laughter, most of it

Accordionist Barry Smith
and his Bavarian band.

originating from a band member who had adopted the suitably Bavarian-style name of Hans for the evening.

The German theme continued into the interval, when we were served with a traditional cold buffet, washed down with half-pint tankards of lager, shandy, cider or soft drinks. Well fed, we reassembled for the second half of the concert, when we needed plenty of energy to engage in some active audience participation as Barry led us in some lively singing. It was an evening to remember and raised a total of £215, for which we were extremely grateful to Barry and his band.

We were in party mood again on Saturday 18th January 1992, when we held a panto-style party at which everyone had to dress as a traditional pantomime character. Cinderella, Snow White, Jack (and his beanstalk), the Ugly Sisters, Prince Charming and Widow Twankey were all represented, and at times it was difficult to guess who was hiding behind the impressive costumes. We also welcomed members of Walsall Spiritualist Church, who joined us for an excellent meal, after which we were entertained by a young couple singing songs from the shows.

****

In stark contrast to so many happy events, January 1993 brought profound sadness. The outstanding medium Gordon Higginson, with whom I had enjoyed a great friendship for more than 40 years, passed suddenly to the higher life and it was my privilege to conduct his funeral. His loss was keenly felt in our church community and we decided to honour him with a special commemorative event on Hydesville Day – 31st March.

The local *Stourbridge News* published an article in advance of the event, which pleased us, since it made the general public aware of some important aspects of Spiritualist history, and the reasons why 31st March is such a significant date in our lives. Here are some extracts from their article:

Stourbridge National Spiritualist Church in the West Midlands is to put on a special event to celebrate Hydesville Day, the memorable day in 1848 on which modern Spiritualism was born.

An inside view of the Fox sisters' Hydesville home
appeared in the local Stourbridge News.

"We are going to commemorate the event on 31ˢᵗ March," said church secretary Mr Roberts. The event, he said would be "in the form of a memorial" for the celebrated medium and former president of the Spiritualists' National Union, Gordon Higginson, who passed earlier this year.

Eric Hatton – he is both president of the church and newly appointed president of the SNU – is organising the proceedings, which will include music and readings on Gordon's life.

It was on that auspicious day 145 years ago, at Hydesville, New York State, USA, that the two Fox sisters, 15-year-old Margaretta and 12-year-old Catherine (known as Katie), first established intelligent conversation with a spirit entity.

The ensuing publicity attracted visitors to the house in droves. 70 or 80 people at a time would crowd into the tiny one-storey cottage in order to witness the strange phenomena.

Home circles were set up in towns far and wide, and within a very short space of time, Spiritualism made a triumphal sweep across America.

In 1852, Boston, Massachusetts medium Mrs W.R. Hayden brought Spiritualism to Britain. Just one year later, at Keighley in Yorkshire, the first Spiritualist church to be established in Great Britain was opened.

****

By this time we had come to the conclusion that our ever-expanding church community needed yet more space, and plans were set in motion to extend the church for a third time. Prior to this we had to raise funds, and, as had been the case with our 1976 extension, church members generously made us interest-free loans which we undertook to repay as soon as possible. We also had various fund-raising events, including concerts and social functions, all of which raised helpful sums. The buy-a-brick scheme which had served us so well in 1976 was reinstated and brought in a considerable amount of money.

I appealed directly to people at various events, asking if they would donate money toward the planned extension, and also asked that if any of them were proposing to make a will, they would consider favouring the church. Looking back, I suppose it was quite cheeky of me to have done that, but that is what I did, and people were very generous in their responses, particularly when we asked them to consider putting a little extra in the collections taken at services.

In addition to our home-grown fund-raising activities, we borrowed some money from the SNU Trust, which was a great help to us. Later, after we had run out of our own money and needed more to complete the work we were undertaking, a most generous gentleman came to our rescue.

Philip Breeze, a generous benefactor to the church.

Philip Breeze had been a member of our church since the passing of his wife in 1983, although they had only come to the church once in her lifetime. She received healing on that occasion, and Philip was so profoundly impressed that he decided to become a member. One evening he came up to me and said: "Eric, I understand you are running out of funds. How are you going to finish the church if you don't have the money?"

He told me that he would bring a cheque the following Sunday, and true to his word he arrived with a cheque for £15,000, which was a great deal of money in those days. Philip's generosity enabled us to finish the building of the church and pay the builders for all the work they had done. Though he is now frail and virtually blind, Philip demonstrates his continuing enthusiasm for the church with regular contributions. He is a wonderful man and we owe him a great debt of gratitude.

In the meantime, as preliminary plans were drawn up by the architect Ken Hodson, our church activities continued as normal and included one particularly noteworthy event – an exhibition in honour of the Spiritualist pioneer Emma Hardinge Britten. It was the brainchild of church member Julie Waters, who did a vast amount of work compiling historical data and assembling various artefacts. The two-day event also included a talk and a re-enactment in period costume of scenes from Emma's life. It was extremely well organised and very much to Julie's credit. Regrettably, she passed away in 2011.

Barry Smith, who had done such a wonderful job for us in 1976, was once again engaged to oversee our building work. He introduced modifications to the architect's plans, all of which made the church what it is today. But prior to the major work starting, preliminary alterations were commenced. Part of the land behind the church was excavated, and the wall behind the rostrum at the far end of the church was demolished and boarded so that we could continue to hold

Harry Saich, vice-president throughout much of the 1990s.

services on a Sunday. Various weekday groups would also be able to keep functioning, though the builders would be working on parts of the church during the week.

This polythene canopy, attached to an outer frame, protected the platform area while work was undertaken on the roof.

So it was that every Saturday my vice-president Harry Saich and I would climb ladders on either side of the church to affix a polythene canopy over the rostrum in order to protect that Sunday's medium from the worst excesses of the weather. To their great credit, Barry Smith and his men had built an outer frame to which we were able to secure the canopy over the exposed area so that we could continue to hold our services there. Though we didn't yet know it, our building programme, which had been proceeding so smoothly, was about to encounter a serious hitch.

Chapter 9

In the course of the excavations, which were behind Prospect House, the house was to be incorporated into the church so as to form part of the church itself. We had decided that the new structures would also extend into the gardens, making the church much wider than before.

When eventually those excavations got under way, the man operating the mechanical digger suddenly became aware that he had hit solid metal. Puzzled, he began to drag it back with the digger, and stared in astonishment as a large well was revealed. Barry Smith was greatly concerned and telephoned me with the news. I in turn contacted Harry Saich and we both went straight to the site.

The well was huge and had been covered with a steel plate.

The well was huge, and had been covered by a steel plate, which was what the digger's blade had encountered. Though we did not know it at the time, the well fed water into an out-building belonging to the house, which had in the distant past been used as a home brewery and laundry. We needed to know how deep it was, so Barry Smith obtained a very long rope, tied a brick to it and lowered it down until it touched the water. He then measured from the top of the well to the rope, marked the place on the rope, and withdrew it from the well.

A mechanical digger crashed into the new church wall while levelling off soft soil, which gave way. Fortunately, little damage was done and only three bricks had to be replaced.

From the floor of the garden to the top of the water in the well was a distance of some thirty feet. But our real concern was about the depth of the well in its entirety. So the brick was lowered once again, until it struck the very bottom of the well. Doing the calculations, we realised that the brick had travelled a further thirty feet down, making the total depth of the well an amazing sixty feet. Needless to say, we weren't sure about the condition of the water, so a bucket was tied to the rope, lowered into the water and drawn up. Although soil had fallen into the well as a result of the excavations, we found that the water was relatively clear and not stagnant. It turned out that the water flowed underneath the church, the car park and the surrounding land.

Extensive work is carried out inside the main church building.

There was no doubt that we had a serious problem. We were so concerned that I decided to contact the borough engineer. He came promptly to the site, and having taken a look at the huge well, declared that there was no way we could cover it up. We would have to fill it in, he said. So we covered it carefully that night, just in case sightseers and nosey parkers came to look down the well and fell in.

The next day, Barry Smith set about ordering vast amounts of stone to be delivered by lorries and tipped into the well. Then steel mesh and a steel grille were fitted towards the top of the well, and covered by concrete. The process was then repeated: more mesh, another grille and then more concrete on top. It was a huge job. Though I can't give a precise figure, there is no doubt that the wholly unexpected episode of the well added a significant amount of money to our bill. Nevertheless, once it was safely filled in and covered we were able to continue with the planned extension, which would otherwise have been impossible.

Looking back on it, there was an interesting side issue to this

Restoration of the roof of the original Gospel Hall building.

A canopy and ornamental columns are added to enhance the façade of the newly extended church.

Part of the newly-fitted church kitchen.

The extended church interior, significantly wider than before.

story. Had we thought of it before we called in the borough engineer, we might have covered up the well secretly, put in a means of drawing off the water and thereby provided bottled Stourbridge Water, which would have been a marvellous source of income for the church. Unfortunately, there was the small matter that all water in the area belongs to the Severn Trent water company!

Following the dramatic saga of the well, building work resumed. Prospect House had originally consisted of four rooms on each of its two storeys and in the early days had been rented out for the princely sum of 12s 6d per week. During the 1976 extension it had been converted into two separate flats, which were let to members of the church.

Now, it underwent a further series of alterations, with the two upstairs rooms being made into one large area. The toilet and bathroom were retained, and on the other side of the staircase we had an office, a room which holds a photocopier, and a storage room for various paraphernalia associated with the church. The garage underneath the house was filled in, and the area over the garage became part of the church extension, forming the vestibule, entrance hall, new ladies', gents' and disabled toilets. A new large and well-equipped kitchen was fitted in the house itself, and behind that new heating boilers were installed to distribute heat efficiently via new pipework throughout the house and church. Both house and church were completely rewired so that there would be no danger of old wiring or heating, with their attendant fire risks, becoming part of the new buildings.

Members of the Floral Group were concerned about where their stands, vases, metal display racks and other equipment would be stored, so we provided them with a dedicated space near the boiler, on condition that they kept their equipment away from the heating apparatus itself, in order to comply with fire regulations.

All in all, the building process had taken ten months to

complete. Both church and house had been transformed and our pleasure in the end result far outweighed the minor inconveniences we had experienced while the work was carried out.

We had hoped that Gordon Higginson would conduct the dedication service for our new extension, just as he had done in 1976. He had expressed a deep desire to be present and rededicate the new church when it was finished, but sadly it was not to be. Following

The beautiful embroidered banner, unveiled at the dedication service.

his passing I became president of the SNU and in August 1994 I conducted the dedication service myself.

Among those present that afternoon was Dorothy Hudson, president of the SNU's District Council, a minister and a very devoted servant of the Union. Tim Horton, SNU treasurer, also attended. The deputy mayor and mayoress of Dudley took part in the proceedings, she unveiling a beautiful 5' by 3' banner embroidered by Leslie Everson-Roberts, incorporating the SNU logo and a representation of our beautiful stained-glass window.

In the evening a congregation of 224 people were privileged to witness an electrifying demonstration of mediumship by Mavis Pittilla, which proved beyond doubt to all present that our loved ones survive beyond physical death.

Medium Mavis Pittilla

The following report of the dedication service, written by Richard Austin, appeared in Issue Four of the *New Communicator.*

Stourbridge Church re-opens in impressive style

Stourbridge National Spiritualist Church, the Church of Spiritualists' National Union President Eric Hatton MSNU was re-opened on 20th August with a large scale re-dedication service attended by over three hundred including many well known in the Spiritualist movement. The Deputy Mayor and Mayoress of Dudley attended.

In just 10 months, the church has been extensively re-built and extended, having been designed by Chartered Architect and SNU director Ken Hodson. As well as seating up to three hundred people, it has many additional rooms and parking for sixty cars. Despite its size, the main body of the church has no columns to obscure the view of the platform.

The work was done despite some interesting problems. A well sixty feet deep was discovered during the excavations.

In a service lasting over two hours, addresses were given by Dorothy Hudson, MSNU, President of West Midlands District Council, Tim Horton MSNU, Treasurer of the Union, Judith Seaman, MSNU Vice-President of the Union and Eric Hatton himself who is also President of the Church. In the evening, Mavis Pittilla CSNU, Senior Tutor of the Arthur Findlay College capped the day with a magnificent demonstration of survival.

Seven flower displays around the Church had each been designed by the Church Flower Group to represent each of the Seven Principles of Spiritualism.

Music played a big part. The hymns, one written by Eric Hatton's sister, were augmented by a Cole Porter duet.

The church has one of the largest memberships in the country with about two hundred and fifty members. It has been their support and enthusiasm which made the work possible. Even on the morning of the service it had looked all but impossible to have the church ready in time, but a team of volunteers pitched in and the work was done.

In the programme for the service, the church committee thanked those who had made it possible with these words:

'In our contribution to the creating of a church where the cultivating of spiritual awareness, the dispensing of solace and healing to any who come in their need, we shall be bringing into practical fruition our aims and ideals.

What greater service to God can we render?'

Only one question remains to be answered: which church will follow suit?

****

At a later date, government legislation was introduced with the aim of making buildings accessible to those who were disabled. To this end, a ramp was constructed in front of the house on the left hand side of the church, which now provides easy wheelchair access to the front doors of the church. The steps on the right-hand side remain.

It had been our original intention to build on special rooms for healing, which would have been attached to the extended church building as it reached the car park. However, when we discovered that this would cost the very considerable sum of £30,000 to accomplish, we realised it was well beyond our means.

Therefore, we decided to provide some form of grassed area behind the church. It is now known as the Memorial Garden and consists of small beds for roses and other flowers. It is a pleasant and peaceful spot where people have often chosen to scatter the

Stourbridge National Spiritualist Church as it is today.

Parts of the newly-created Memorial Garden.

ashes of their loved ones.

Before ending this account of the 1994 building works, I must
pay tribute to the skill, hard work and kindness of Barry Smith,
who was present at the dedication service. To his great credit, Barry
also provided us with a display board inside the church entrance
hall, and another fixed to the outside wall, on which we announce
details of our weekly services and speakers.

Chapter 10

As the building work neared completion, concerns had been expressed about whether we might run out of money. Additional expenses had been incurred because of problems relating to the discovery of the well, and the treasurer Ted Turner was also worried that there would be insufficient funds for the upkeep of a bigger church. So it was that in September 1994 a '200 Club' was inaugurated. Church members and friends paid for a share in the club, and each month there would be a draw for three prize-winners. The club was managed by Margaret Bradley, Mary Simmonds, Marjorie and Harry Saich, who all rose to the challenge of recruiting sufficient members to make the scheme a success. By September 1998 we had raised £4,000 and were well on the way towards £5,000.

The world-famous Reading Phoenix Choir.

It was music all the way as we sought to raise further funds to cover the cost of our building programme. Over the next few years we were privileged to welcome numerous musicians and singers to our newly extended church, and none more so than the world-renowned Reading Phoenix Choir, who first visited us on 30th

September 1995. My good friend Norman Morris was the choir's founder and conductor so the event was a particular pleasure for me.

The concert opened dramatically, in complete silence, with the solitary entrance of Norman's wife, Rosie, a choir member and soprano soloist, who came slowly up the centre aisle of the church, stepped on to the platform and sang the first verse of an unaccompanied

Choral conductor Norman Morris.

song, *Beauty for Ashes.* As she came to the chorus, the other members of the choir entered through the doors at either side of the church, and also through the front entrance and middle aisle, singing as they walked along in procession. As the chorus finished, they stood as still as statues, facing in whatever direction they had reached, until such time as Rosie had sung the second verse. They then joined in the second chorus and moved into their positions on the platform. The full choir was then assembled, and gave us a wonderful concert. The place was absolutely packed, even the extra seats in the extension area which is now known as the social room. The £1,000 proceeds from ticket sales were shared equally between the church and the choir.

Valerie Masterson C.B.E.

Another outstanding fund-raising event took the form of a high-profile gala concert with a very distinguished guest performer. It was the brainchild of Leslie Everson-Roberts, who was church secretary at the time. Leslie prevailed upon his friend, the world-famous operatic soprano Valerie Masterson C.B.E., to come and sing for us. Valerie had sung in all the world's major opera houses and concert halls and we felt privileged that she had generously agreed to donate her services to us.

Pianist and organist Michael Thompson.

She was joined by Helen Landis, an excellent contralto who had appeared in musicals in London and the provinces, plus two very fine local singers, Don Derby and his son Jonathan. All four were accompanied by the pianist Leslie Sykes. Once again, the church was absolutely packed, and you could have heard a pin drop as Valerie regaled her audience with Schubert's haunting *Ave Maria*, Adolph Adam's *The Holy City* and other traditional songs including the much-loved favourite, *Bless this House* – a most appropriate choice for our brand new church.

Helen Landis performed a selection of numbers from *South Pacific*, plus songs by Grieg and Johann Strauss. She also gave us a most dramatic performance of the famous *Habanera* from Bizet's opera *Carmen*.

As well as performing individual solos, father and son Don and Jonathan Darby joined forces for Offenbach's popular *Gendarmes' Duet*, much to the delight of the audience. Almost £1,500 was raised from this very special event, and all of it went towards offsetting our debt for the building of the extensions.

Other concerts were given by Michael Thompson, a fine pianist and organist who by this time had been associated with the church for many years and often accompanied our services. On

84

one occasion he was joined by another fine pianist, Frank Moore, and the two of them gave a musical evening at which they invited various others to contribute. The audience greatly enjoyed the programme, which included piano duets, and also a piano and organ duo performed by Michael and Frank.

Over the years there have been innumerable concerts and other events featuring local artists, including our own organist, Geoff Heath, who entertained us on a number of occasions at church dinners. At one point, Geoff even turned his hand to learning the piano accordion, playing briefly for us at a social event. It is certainly true to say that we have been blessed to have a number of gifted musicians within our church community.

****

The year 1998 saw another in our series of flower festivals, which took place during the weekend of 4th to 7th July. It was in aid of the Mary Stevens Hospice, and we were delighted that Councillor Fred Hunt, deputy mayor of Dudley, agreed to open it for us. The theme was 'World of Colour', and as always the floral displays were stunning, depicting each colour of the spectrum, arranged in company with its harmonising colours.

On the Saturday, we enjoyed an evening of music and poetry and on the Sunday I conducted an afternoon naming ceremony, which was followed by an evening of psychic art with Su Wood and Heather Hatton. Healing was available at various times during the weekend and many took the opportunity to experience it. On Monday evening we were treated to a marvellous performance by Barry Smith

Psychic artist Su Wood.

who, as I explained earlier, is not only an excellent builder but a celebrated accordionist who has performed for many well-known people, including the Queen Mother, to whom he was twice personally introduced.

We were also privileged to have a visit from the award-winning Canoldir Choir of Birmingham, which is made up of a number of prominent Birmingham musicians, doctors and other professional people. Amongst them was Dr Charles Gwynn, husband of one of our church members, who was instrumental in arranging their concert for us.

There are times in life when an experience leaves one without words which can adequately reflect the quality, value or impact it has on one's senses. The return visit of the magnificent Reading Phoenix Choir on 26th September 1998 was just such an occasion for me and many others. Once again the church was absolutely packed, even into the extension, though earlier that evening we had feared for audience numbers because of a heavy downpour.

Every piece on the varied programme was performed without the aid of sheet music or a book, but with consummate excellence and ease, proving once again that the choir is indeed one of the best in the UK, and probably in many another country. I should also mention that not only did the fifty choir members squeeze themselves into the limited accommodation that we had upstairs in the house as was, and into the kitchen area too; they also changed their garments completely during the interval. It was a marvellous evening, a privilege for all who attended, and we made a huge profit from their visit. The choir continues with great success today, despite the sad loss of Norman Morris, who passed on in 2010.

Chapter 11

The memorable millennium celebration party at Stourbridge church.

The new millennium provided cause for great celebration around the world, and Stourbridge church was no exception. Our social committee went to great lengths to organise a splendid party, for which long tables were laid out in the main body of the church. A festive colour scheme of silver and black was reflected in the special tablecloths, serviettes, plates and cups which adorned the tables, while similarly-coloured garlands were festooned around the church. Amid an atmosphere of high good humour, many of the hundred people present donned hats and masks in matching colours while children amused themselves with blow trumpets and whistles. A sit-down meal was served and we enjoyed some excellent entertainment from pianist Michael Thompson and a local singer named Judith Farmer. I sang myself, and we all joined in some very cheerful community singing.

Celebration of a quieter kind came with a further flower festival from 24th to 26th June 2000. Entitled *Journey through the years*, it illustrated in floral arrangements the various stages of life from birth through school-days and teens, to middle age, retirement and beyond. Special life events were also depicted in flowers, including weddings, golden weddings, twenty-first birthdays and many others.

Debra Shipley MP

We were privileged to have the festival opened by Debra Shipley, who had been elected MP for Stourbridge in 1997.

Debra was highly delighted by the floral displays and expressed great enthusiasm for what she had seen. Indeed, she stayed for nearly an hour after the opening ceremony, simply talking with us and admiring the designs. Interestingly, during

Medium Maureen Murnan

our conversation she told me that her grandmother had been a Spiritualist. The medium and speaker for that weekend was Maureen Murnan, and on the Monday we enjoyed an evening with Tommy Mundon, a celebrated Black Country comedian with whom I have been friends for almost 60 years. Tommy has graced television screens, public

The well-loved Black Country comedian Tommy Mundon.

halls, theatres (and our church) for decades and is popular even today. Once again, all proceeds from the event were donated to the Mary Stevens Hospice in Stourbridge.

It was party time again in June 2002 as from one end of the UK to the other celebrations were held in honour of the Queen's Golden Jubilee. As with the millennium party, long tables stretched from the social room into the main body of the church, this time bedecked with patriotic red, white and blue cloths and garlands, a theme echoed in the plates, cups and other tableware. A packed church enjoyed a cold buffet as flags were waved, trumpets blown, and patriotic songs such as *Rule Britannia* and *Roll out the Barrel* were sung. It was a memorable and fitting celebration of the Queen's fifty-year reign.

The next flower festival followed hard on the heels of our jubilee party and was opened by the mayor of Dudley, Councillor Margaret Wilson. It ran from Saturday 13th to Monday 15th July and was entitled 'Flowers from around the world'. All proceeds were donated to Talking Newspapers for the Blind. On the Sunday afternoon of the festival there was a naming service in the church, which I conducted. It was followed on the Monday by an evening of psychic art with mediums Su Wood and Jean Kelford. Some time later Su was joined by the medium Janet Parker for one of several propaganda meetings held in the first few years of the new millennium.

In September 2006 we had the pleasure of welcoming the renowned Brazilian spirit artist Jose Medrado to the church. What makes Medrado's mediumship so unusual is that he becomes entranced while standing upright in front of a large table, enabling various well-known artists of the past – including Renoir, Monet, Manet, Degas, van Gogh, Matisse and Cézanne – to paint through his hands, which are encased in surgical gloves.

One of the most remarkable things is that although the many tubes of paint are laid out on the table in front of him, and Medrado's eyes remain closed during his trance state, the various colours are picked up and smeared appropriately by hand on the canvasses that are offered to him one after another by his assistant Solange. I myself had purchased those canvasses, which remained sealed until the demonstration was about to begin, thus removing any chance of fraudulently pre-prepared pictures. At times, the paints were smeared on top of one another until such time as a picture of extraordinary beauty was fashioned.

Those in the audience who were experienced in painting techniques were astounded by another aspect of the work, since it is well known in artistic circles that you cannot put one oil colour on top of another before several hours have elapsed, in order that the first can dry. And yet here was this remarkable outpouring of spirit influence which defied all conventional wisdom in so far as painting was concerned.

The whole of this demonstration, which was conducted in broad daylight, was projected onto a large screen for all to be able to see clearly what was happening.

Perhaps the most astonishing aspect of Medrado's demonstrations concerns the time taken to produce a finished painting – on this occasion between 5 minutes 42 seconds for a Renoir and 10 minutes 17 seconds for a van Gogh.

At the conclusion, as Medrado rested for a short while, the paintings – which had been propped up to dry in various parts of the church – were sold off by auction. Some of them fetched as much as £500, and all the proceeds, without the deduction of any expenses for Medrado, went to support the homes for orphans and battered women that he has founded in his native Brazil.

Such is the respect for him in that country, and in America, that he gives frequent radio and television broadcasts. Again, all money raised from those is donated to the homes. Medrado is a charming and spiritual man, whose work is always carried out with modesty and humility. We were privileged to have a further visit from him in 2007.

Lynda Waltho MP

The very last of our flower festivals took place in 2006, when Lynda Waltho, who had succeeded Debra Shipley as MP for Stourbridge the previous year, opened the proceedings, expressing great pleasure at being invited to do so. As an aside, I should mention that when I was first introduced to Lynda by Councillor Fred Hunt, he told me something that amazed me. During his year of office as mayor, he and his wife had attended many functions as principal representatives of the borough, but apparently the only church that had ever given them anything for their presence was our own.

As I look back over almost twenty years of flower festivals, I am struck by the fact that each and every one of them was spectacular in its own way and did great credit to our church. Perhaps, though, it is the 1981 event that stands out most clearly in my memory, since its displays were designed to reflect the International Year of Disabled Persons and had an added poignancy which brought something particularly special to the event.

My overriding memory of each and every festival is that the displays were vivid and vibrant in colour. The whole church was awash with colour and each arrangement was unique and remarkable. I have seen many floral festivals in other churches, and maybe I am biased, but I have never seen any that I believe compared with those we held. Perhaps because our church was relatively small by comparison with an Anglican or Methodist church, our displays were relatively more compact and the flowers were that much more a panorama of colour.

Mary Simmonds, organiser and talented designer
of the more recent flower festivals.

Over the years the composition of the floral group has necessarily changed somewhat, but the backbone membership has remained the same. One must pay tribute to Mary Simmonds, the organiser and designer of the more recent floral festivals, all of which have been extremely successful and brought great delight and pleasure to the people of Stourbridge who have chosen to come and view them.

****

In 2009 I suffered a severe bout of ill-health, culminating in major surgery. Throughout my long period of convalescence church affairs were overseen by my very capable vice-president Laraine Killarney, who visited me regularly and kept me informed of events. Towards the end of that year I was relieved to feel well enough to take up the reins again. Sadly, by late 2010 my health had deteriorated in other ways, and with considerable sadness I decided that the time had come for me to step down as president.

*Laraine Killarney, unanimously elected
president of Stourbridge Church.*

After almost seven decades of association with the church it was not an easy decision to make, but I knew that it was the right one. Accordingly, at the church's annual general meeting on 16th March 2011 a new president was unanimously elected and I was very much touched to be offered the specially-created role of Honorary President.

The editor of *Psychic News* attended that meeting, and this is her report:

Eric Hatton steps down at Stourbridge

The Spiritualist movement's best known church president has stepped down after almost fifty years in the hot seat.

At Stourbridge church's annual general meeting on 16th March, I watched from the back as members listened intently to Minister Eric Hatton, also Honorary President of the

Spiritualists' National Union, while he delivered his final presidential address. He urged members to preserve the highest possible standards of mediumship and philosophy in the future, adding that these things were crucial to the success and credibility of Spiritualism. His strongest and most passionate plea concerned the importance of maintaining "the harmony" of the church community.

Eric's association with the church goes back to 1947, when, following the death of his much loved brother, his quest for survival evidence led him to attend a demonstration by Gordon Higginson. Not only did that demonstration provide Eric with evidence so outstanding that it would change the course of his life, it also marked the beginning of a deep friendship between the two men which was to last until Gordon's passing in 1993.

Eric became a church member in 1948 and the rest is history. By 1949 he had become church secretary, and following a period as vice-president was unanimously elected president in 1963.

Under Eric's leadership, carried out with the dedicated support of his late wife Heather, Stourbridge National Spiritualist Church became a beacon for Spiritualism, hosting the very best mediums and speakers. Albert Best, Doris Collins, Doris Stokes, Robin Stevens, Sally Ferguson, Mary Duffy and Gordon Higginson were among a plethora of outstanding mediums who graced its platform on a regular basis. That tradition of excellence continues today with visits from such gifted mediums as Gerard Smith, Eileen Davies, Robert Goodwin, Jackie Wright, John Conway, Andy Byng and others.

During his long presidency Eric has also overseen three major renovations and extensions to the church, which today is a warm, inviting and well-equipped space, frequently full to capacity. Over the past few years it has been my privilege to attend services at Stourbridge on numerous occasions and there is no doubt that a uniquely special atmosphere exists within its walls, due in significant measure to Eric's devoted service over so many years. Even when 150 people are present he will move around the church greeting and speaking with each one individually, a gesture guaranteed to make them feel welcome and valued.

In recent years Eric has suffered several periods of severe ill health and has at times struggled valiantly to fulfil his many and varied commitments within the Spiritualist movement. I put it to him that it must have been a very difficult decision to give up the presidency of a church which has long been so closely identified with him that it is frequently referred to as "his" church.

"It has never been my church," he told me. "I feel very sad about stepping down. I would have liked to be able to continue, not for the length of time I have been president, but because of my devotion to the church itself. However, I will continue to be involved and to assist our new president in any way I can."

So who is to take over from Eric? Members have elected Laraine Killarney, who has been one of Stourbridge's two vice-presidents for the past four years. I asked her how she felt about following in Eric's footsteps.

"I find this a sad occasion as – largely for health reasons – Eric is standing down as president," she told me. "Our church is well known far and wide for its high standards of Spiritualism and the evidence it provides. Eric has been my mentor for the past four years and I am proud to follow in his footsteps as president. I cannot be another Eric but with all the help and training he has graciously passed on to me I will endeavour to keep the same excellent standards that he and Heather have achieved."

Speaking at the close of the AGM, Laraine announced that Eric had been asked to accept the title of Honorary President in recognition of his long and outstanding service to the church.

This was greeted with lengthy applause and an emotional standing ovation.

****

Under Laraine's presidency Stourbridge National Spiritualist Church continues to thrive. She is supported by vice-presidents Geoff Jones and Kath Garrad, a dedicated committee and a loyal membership, as together they take the proud tradition of Stourbridge Spiritualism into the future.

*

Within us we have a hope which always walks in front of our present narrow experience; it is the undying faith in the infinite in us; it will never accept any of our disabilities as a permanent fact; it sets no limit to its own scope; it dares to assert that it has oneness with God; and its wildest dreams come true every day.

For our life, like a river, strikes its banks not to find itself closed in by them, but to realise anew every moment that it has its unending opening towards the sea.

Rabindrath Tagore
from *Sadhana*

Appendices

1. Church Officers

2. Committee Members

3. Church Healers

4. Mediums who have served the church

1. Church Officers

Presidents

Mr Trussell
Mr Guest
Eric Wright
Percy Brown
Major Vic Mound
Eric Hatton
Muriel Foster
Eric Hatton
Laraine Killarney

Secretaries

Albert Jones
Eric Hatton
Betty Dunster
Muriel Foster
Cissie Shaw
Kath Garrad
Trevene Highfield

Vice-Presidents

Mary (Mickey) Wright
Clarrie Gauden
Isobel Pugh
Graham Dann
John Edwards
Cissie Shaw
James Grainger
Ron Pratt
Robin Chubb
Harry Saich
Mary Edwards
Laraine Killarney
Geoff Jones
Kath Garrad

Treasurers

James Foxhall
Ted Turner
Eric Arnold
Cissie Shaw
Mike Rumble
John Rickwood
Trevene Highfield

Members Secretaries

Albert Jones
Priscilla Williams
Joyce Bate
June Evans Tovey
Heather Hatton
Peggy Baber
Mary Simmonds
Jean Jones

Speakers Secretaries

Albert Jones
Eric Hatton
Ron Pratt
Heather Hatton
Linda Bonehill
Lynda Rawlings

Social Committee

Joyce Bate
Graham Bonehill
Linda Bonehill
Albert Buckley
Robert Dangerfield
Mary Dutton
Lynne Edwards
Sandra Elwell
Muriel Foster
Brian Franklin
Heather Hatton
Tracey Holland
Geoff Jones
Jean Jones
Laraine Killarney
Ron Pratt
Marjorie Saich
Jo Smith
Val Smith
Ted Turner
Ann-Marie Vale
Phyllis Walker
Brett Wood

Organists

Albert Jones
J. Smith
Audrey Wyatt
Sid Wallbank
Lucy Hall
George Ellis
Bernard Bache
Frank Moore
Jeremy Drew
Michael Thompson
Geoff Heath

2. Committee Members
(in alphabetical order)

Carol Arnold
Eric Arnold
Peggy Baber
Joyce Bate
Chris Bennett
J. Biggs
Mark Boulter
Mike Bowen
Norman Bowen
Margaret Bradley
Percy Brown
Albert Buckley
Rene Cannell
Annette Chubb
Robin Chubb
Arnold Compson
Graham Dann
Marjorie Dudley
Robert Dudley
Mary Dutton
John Edwards
Mary Edwards
Dennis Elwell
Sandra Elwell
June Evans Tovey
Leslie Everson Roberts
Muriel Foster
Gladys Foxhall
James Foxhall

Richard Friday
Kath Garrad
Jack Gibbons
Betty Gosling/Pryse/
Dunster
James Grainger
Stuart Harris
Eric Hatton
Heather Hatton
Bobbie Hickman
Trevene Highfield
Tracey Holland
Reg Horton
Albert Jones
Geoff Jones
Jean Jones
Laraine Killarney
Olive Large
Major Vic Mound
Pat Parry
Alan Perry
Bill Perry
Hilda Perry
Jack Powell
Ron Pratt
Mary Priest
Isobel Pugh
Lynda Rawlings
John Rickwood

Mike Rumble
Harry Saich
Marjorie Saich
Janet Seddon
Joyce Sharples
Cissie Shaw
Marjorie Simmons
Mary Simmonds
Carole Singer
Sylvia Stanier
Jack Steadman
Gary Taylor
Michael Thompson

Gladys Tonks
David Tooby
Alice Tudor
Ted Turner
Phyllis Walker
Angela Wallbank
Norah Weston
Mr & Mrs Whittle
Priscilla William
Mrs (Welsh) Williams
Su Wood
Mary (Mickey) Wright
David Young

3. Church Healers
(in alphabetical order)

Carol Arnold
Chris Bennett*
Mark Boulter*
Norman Bowen
Annette Chubb
Robin Chubb*
Arnold Compson
Graham Dann
Leslie Frayne
Barbara Frisby*
James Grainger*
Eric Hatton*
Heather Hatton*
Reg Horton
Albert Lewis*
Janet Marsh
Dorothy Marshall
Keith Meager
Mary Priest
Lynda Rawlings
John Rickwood
Harry Saich
Janet Seddon
Terry Sharples
Cissie Shaw
Jessica Shead
Marjorie Simmonds
Jack Steadman
Gary Taylor
Jeannette Wingfield

* Healing leader

4. Mediums who have served the church
(in alphabetical order)

Michael Bagan
Ron Baker
Peter Bancroft
Ray Barden
Harold Barnett
Chris Batchelor
Harold Baxter
Peter Bevan
Marian Bishop
John Blackwood
Leah Bond
Ray Bordes
Sylvia Bowel
Betty Bowles
Grace Boyes
Paul Brereton
Minnie Bridges
Darren Brittain
David Bruton
Mollie Bryant
Charles Bullen
Linda Bullock
Megan Burroughs
Frank Burton
Andrew Byng
Pat Campbell
Joseph Capstack
Bob/Stella Clarke
Ronald Cockershall
Martin Colclough
David Cole
John Conway
Terry Cotterill
Lynette Coulston

Sidney Crocker
Aileen Davies
Eileen Davies
Hugh Davis
Margaret Davis
Christopher Denton
Eamonn Downey
Les Driver
Mary Duffy
Helen Duncan (1937)
Brenda Ebner
Glyn Edwards
George Evans
Sally Ferguson
Gladys Fieldhouse
Will Ford
Diana Fox Spencer
Maud Foxhall
Don Galloway
Donald Gill
Joyce Gobbett
Robert Goodwin
Horace Green
Sheila Green
Eddie Greenyer
Kathy Grindy
Dorne Hall
Lena Hands
Jill Harland
Roberta Harris
Marjorie Hathaway
Heather Hatton
Karen Haycock
Geoffrey Haywood

Marjorie/Janet Hebblethwaite
Ada Herbert
Fannie Higginson
Gordon Higginson
Steve Holbrook
Maria Hope Clarke
Lilian Hudson
Margaret Hurdman
Paul Jacobs
Simon James
J. Jolly
Kath Jones
Richard Jones
Rita/Derek Jones
Jean Kelford
Vi Kipling
Bobbie Kovacs
Lee Lacey
Joan Lambert
Bill Landis
Jenny Larder
Brenda Lawrence
Stuart Lawson
Len Lobban
Clive Lloyd
Laura Lloyd
Bryan Lynch
Nan Mackenzie
Mary Maclean
George McAllister
Angela McGee
Angela McInnes
Nan McKenzie

Tom/Shirley Mair
Alice Mirfin
Sandrea Mosses
Gaye Muir
Maureen Murnan
Brenda Newell
Queenie Nixon
Stephen O'Brien
Danny O'Connor
Glynis Owen
Gordon Pamely
Yvonne Pamely
Janet Parker
Lallie Paxton
Florence Pearce
Margaret Pearson
Hilda Perry
Connie Phillips
M. Pickering
J. Pilkington
Mavis Pittilla
Muriel Plimmer
Sue Presley
Margaret Priest
Bill Redmond
Patricia Redmond
Betty Reeves
Dorothy Ridges
Eileen Roberts
Brian Robertson
Helen Rollinson
Hardiman Scott
Judith Seaman
Vi Shakespeare

Joyce Sharples
Kath Shirley
Brenda Simpson
Jean Skinner
Gerard Smith
Matthew Smith
Joyce Steadman
Dora Stephen
Robin Stevens
Donna Stewart
Alf Swann
Albert Taylor
Nella Taylor
Billy Thomas
Pauline Thornton

Eva Upton
Ann-Marie Vale
Shirley Vinnicombe
Betty Wakeling
Stephen Wakeling
Arthur Whyman
Joe Wilcox
Val Williams
Ray Williamson
Su Wood
Nan Worley
Jackie Wright
Mary (Mickey) Wright/Ellis
Leonard Young
Martin Young